Science Tools

Rulers and Tape Measures

Lisa J. Amstutz

a Capstone company — publishers for children

Raintree is an imprint of Capstone Global Library Limited, a company incorporated in England and Wales having its registered office at 264 Banbury Road, Oxford, OX2 7DY – Registered company number: 6695582

www.raintree.co.uk
myorders@raintree.co.uk

Text © Capstone Global Library Limited 2020
The moral rights of the proprietor have been asserted.

All rights reserved. No part of this publication may be reproduced in any form or by any means (including photocopying or storing it in any medium by electronic means and whether or not transiently or incidentally to some other use of this publication) without the written permission of the copyright owner, except in accordance with the provisions of the Copyright, Designs and Patents Act 1988 or under the terms of a licence issued by the Copyright Licensing Agency, Barnard's Inn, 86 Fetter Lane, London, EC4A 1EN (www.cla.co.uk). Applications for the copyright owner's written permission should be addressed to the publisher.

Edited by Anna Butzer
Designed by Cynthia Della-Rovere
Picture research by Kelly Garvin
Production by Tori Abraham
Originated by Capstone Global Library Limited

ISBN 978 1 4747 6930 3 (hardback)
ISBN 978 1 4747 6948 8 (paperback)

British Library Cataloguing in Publication Data
A full catalogue record for this book is available from the British Library

Acknowledgements
We would like to thank the following for permission to reproduce photographs: Alamy/Myrleen Pearson, 9; Capstone Press/Karon Dubke, cover, 1 (top), 5, 7, 11 (bottom), 13, 15, 17, 19, 21; iStockphoto/akiyoko, 3; Shutterstock: Kaspri, 3 (b), nikshor, 1 (b), 11 (t), Tatyaby, 21 (left), topseller, 21 (middle), Utekhina Anna, 21 (right)
Design elements: Shutterstock: Alina G, Astarina, Fafarumba, happy_fox_art, Lorelyn Medina, mhatzapa, Netkoff, Nikitina Karina, olllikeballoon, PedroNevesDesign, Visual Generation.

Every effort has been made to contact copyright holders of material reproduced in this book. Any omissions will be rectified in subsequent printings if notice is given to the publisher.

All the internet addresses (URLs) given in this book were valid at the time of going to press. However, due to the dynamic nature of the internet, some addresses may have changed, or sites may have changed or ceased to exist since publication. While the author and publisher regret any inconvenience this may cause readers, no responsibility for any such changes can be accepted by either the author or the publisher.

Printed and bound in India

Contents

The right tool 4
Rulers and tape measures 6
Reading rulers and tape measures 10
Let's measure! 14
Safety first! 18

    Glossary 22
    Find out more 23
    Websites 23
    Index 24

The Right Tool

How tall is a flower? How far around is a tree trunk? To find out, you need a tool. A ruler or a tape measure will do the job!

Rulers and Tape Measures

A ruler is straight.

It is made of a hard material.

It is good for measuring things that are small and straight.

A tape measure is longer than a ruler.

It can measure things that are not straight.

It can bend around curves.

Reading rulers and tape measures

Rulers and tape measures have marks on them. Some of these marks show inches. Other marks show centimetres.

inches

centimetres

Rulers help you to draw a straight line. They can help you draw triangles and squares. You can measure the four sides of a square to make sure each side is the same length.

Let's measure!

Let's measure a pencil.

Lay the pencil next to the ruler.

Line up the pencil point with the zero. Then read the number at the end of the rubber. This pencil is nearly 19 centimetres long.

Let's measure a ball. Put the tab of a tape measure on the middle line. Wrap the tape around the ball. Read the number where the ends meet. This ball is 76 centimetres round.

Safety first!

Some tape measures have a spring inside. It makes them roll up fast. Zip! Keep your fingers away from the tape's edge.

Look around!

What can you measure?

Which tool will you use?

21

Glossary

centimetre a unit of metric length measurement, equal to 0.39 inches

inch a unit of length measurement, equal to 2.54 centimetres

material the thing that something is made of

measure to find out the size of something

spring a tightly twisted piece of metal that can be squeezed or stretched but always returns to its former shape

tab the small metal piece at the end of a tape measure

tool something used to make work easier